F. Scott Fitzgerarid

Pablo Picasso

Walt Disney

Ben

Robin Williams

Gwen Stefani

John Lennon

Leonardo da Vinci

Tommy Hilfiger

John Eccles

Dear Reader,

This book does not seek to deny that there are challenges or difficulties with being dyslexic. It simply wishes to offer hope, that good things can and do come from thinking differently.

Enjoy,
Sarah

Copyright:

Published by Sarah Prestidge

ISBN 9780473574888 (Softcover - POD Amazon)

FINDING MY SUPERPOWER

A book for dyslexic thinkers

By Sarah Prestidge
Illustrated by Kauri Finlay

Ben has dyslexia. That is a
hard word to say!

There are lots of things that Ben finds tricky, like reading and spelling. This sometimes makes him feel sad.

One day a teacher told him about Dyslexia
Superpowers. The teacher told Ben that...

Jamie Oliver's superpower is that he can
cook really yummy food that
people like to eat.

Steve Jobs can think of new ideas.

Lots of dyslexic people found school hard, but some became great leaders and even presidents.

Other people's superpower is
being great at sports.

Some dyslexic thinkers became amazing scientists and discovered all kinds of new things.

Others got prizes for finding out how
to make the world better.

Acting is some people's superpower.

While others are amazing singers
or fashion designers.

Some people with dyslexia who
found reading and writing tricky
even wrote books!

Or made movies.

Others became incredible artists...
Or designed motorbikes.

Other people's superpower was
becoming an entrepreneur.

Sometimes it is hard to find your superpower. But that's ok because one day you will, and you may...

Make people laugh...

Build the tallest tower...

Invent awesome
computer games...

Create the greatest
fun park...

Solve big problems...

Encourage people to change...

Run the fastest time...

Design the longest bridge...

Paint the next Mona Lisa...

Play a role in changing the world to make it a better place.

And that will be awesome because the
world needs you and your superpower!

Dyslexic thinkers listed in order as they appear in the book:

Jamie Oliver – Chef

Steve Jobs – Co-founder of Apple

John F Kennedy, George Washington, and George W Bush – American Presidents

Jessica Watson – Youngest person to sail around the world

Magic Johnson – Professional Basketball Player

Chris Robshaw – English Rugby Captain

Muhammad Ali – Professional Boxer

Galileo Galilei – Astronomer

Stephen Hawking – Mathematician & Physicist

Thomas Edison – Inventor

Maggie Aderin – Space Scientist

Alexander Graham Bell – Scientist & Inventor

Jacques Dubochet, Pierre Curie, Carol W. Greider,
Dr. Archer Martin, John Eccles – Nobel Peace Prizes Winners

Keira Knightley, Whoopi Goldberg, Jennifer Aniston, Salma Hayek,
Orlando Bloom, Keanu Reeves, Robin Williams – Actors & Actresses

Gwen Stefani, John Lennon – Musicians

Tommy Hilfiger – Fashion Designer

Agatha Christie, F. Scott Fitzgerarld, Dav Pilkey,
Tom McLaughlin, John Irving – Authors

Walt Disney, Steven Spielberg – Movie Directors

Pablo Picasso, Leonardo da Vinci – Artists

John Britten – Inventor

Richard Branson, Theo Paphitis – Entrepreneurs

Whoopi Goldberg

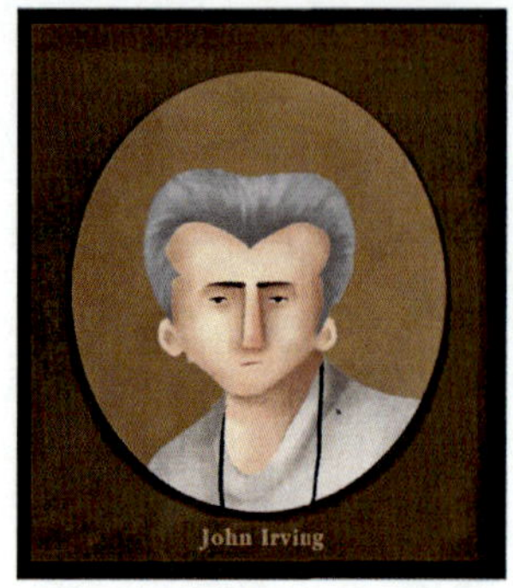
John Irving

Richard Branson

John Britten

Jennifer Aniston

Keanu Reeves

Theo Paphitis

Dav Pilkey

Tom McLaughlin

Salma Hayck

Thomas Edison

Made in United States
North Haven, CT
20 November 2022

26974598R10018